Heavenly Fire

This small book of poems is more than poetry. It is a window into the life of a man who has been a pathfinder for Quakers. His other books of philosophy, theology, history, sermons, and autobiography also reflect the life of this giant. But this volume gives us a uniquely penetrating peak into his soul. It goes from being whimsical to vulnerable, from being lofty to pedestrian, and throughout we see painful honesty. Through this poetic window, we see the life of a tenderly romantic husband, a grounded philosopher, a patient father, a loyal friend, a playful grandfather, and a compassionate pastor. But we also see a brother regretting detachment from his sister, an older man longing for companionship, and a frail human fighting temptations and acknowledging weakness.
These latter glimpses do not negate his gigantic stride, but instead they help us relate to his experiences and they invite us to follow him, walking the path that has "been tended with love."

Corey W. Beals
assistant professor of philosophy and religion
George Fox University

Heavenly Fire
AND OTHER POEMS

by Arthur O. Roberts

BARCLAY
PRESS

HEAVENLY FIRE
and other poems by Arthur O. Roberts

Published by
Barclay Press
Newberg, OR 97132
www.barclaypress.com

ISBN 978-1-59498-011-4

also by Arthur O. Roberts

THE SACRED ORDINARY
Sermons and Addresses

PRAYERS AT TWILIGHT
Prayers that capture the variety of questions and concerns surrounding death

EXPLORING HEAVEN
What Great Christian Thinkers Tell Us about Our Afterlife with God

LET THE SPIRIT SOAR
Mayoral poems of Arthur O. Roberts

LOOK CLOSELY AT THE CHILD
Christmas Poems

MESSENGERS OF GOD
The Sensuous Side of Spirituality

DRAWN BY THE LIGHT
Autobiographical Reflections

BACK TO SQUARE ONE
Turning Losses into Spiritual Gains

SUNRISE AND SHADOW

LISTEN TO THE LORD

MOVE OVER, ELIJAH

Contents

Tribute to Animals

Tributes to Friends

Tributes to Family

Tributes to Fern

Tributes to Grandchildren and Great-grandchildren

Tributes to Places

Tributes to Play

Tributes to Life In Particular

Tributes to God's Grace

Epilogue

Preface

With a few exceptions, as noted, this collection consists of poems not previously published in book form. My earlier books of poetry include: *Listen to the Lord*, *Sunrise and Shadow*, *Look Closely at the Child*, *Let the Spirit Soar*, and *Prayers at Twilight*. Other books that include my poems are: *Move Over, Elijah*; *Drawn by the Light*; *Messengers of God*; *The Wit and Wisdom of Jack Willcuts*; *Exploring Heaven*; and *The Sacred Ordinary*. I also wrote the lyrics for three musicals—*Children of the Light*, *Jonah ben Amittai*, and *Emmaus Road*.

A granddaughter, Heidi Rogers, as a child offered this tribute to her grandfather, Christmas, 1985. She exaggerated my height, which I accept as a metaphoric tribute—love induced—and choose her poem to preface this collection. Thank you, Heidi!

Papa

Born on a farm in Idaho,
he's six feet five
with a shiny head.
He carves wood
and makes it nicer.
He teaches forever
with his writing.
His poems are about Alaska,
Eskimos, his children,
his grandchildren,
and his love of God.

Love, Heidi

Tributes to Animals

A Touch by the Spirit

Thank you, Lord Creator,
for all creatures of the earth
who grace our fields and homes,
and bless us by their presence.

Bless the wild birds and beasts
with whom we compete for a place
called home. We forgive their trespass
as they forgive ours.

Bless these animals whose lives
are bound to ours, who serve us
in many ways, as we serve them.
Lord, we cherish these companions.

To keep the earth a shared space
for creatures great and small
is no easy task for human stewards.
Grant us wisdom, Lord Creator.

Yes, we seek wisdom, Lord—
and a touch by the Holy Spirit.

Loyalty

After seventy years I fondly recall Ted,
a large collie dog of childhood years.
Such a loyal and loving companion!
Ted would pull me about in a little red wagon.
He helped bring in the cows for milking
and kept me company on summer days
when Papa sent me to weed the cornfield.

Ted didn't criticize my mistakes or frown
at my stupidity. He just wagged his tail,
licked my hand, rested beside me on the lawn.
Oh, sometimes we need reproof and correction
and instruction in right living, as the Bible says.
Parents, teachers, pastors, and special friends
often perform these functions, and rightly so.

But we also need folks who, like my dog Ted,
remain cheerfully loyal to us, day after day,
in pleasant and in difficult circumstances,
in spite of sins, goofs, and shortcomings,
who demonstrate through smiles, hugs,
thoughtful gifts, and encouraging words
that loyalty is an essential part of love.

Joyful Eagle

I give tribute to Eagle, a dappled gray Morgan.
How he hated it when, needing extra horsepower
for farm work, we threw the harness on him:
His body sagged, his ears slumped, his head drooped.
"Don't put me through this!" he seemed to say.
But with the saddle, now that was a different story!
Head held high, tail a-twitch, he could hardly wait
for me to cinch up the girth, grab the bridle reins,
and mount. Wow! How he loved to gallop
across the desert above our Idaho farm!

Eagle epitomizes sheer joy, like Raphael Nadal
playing tennis. Have you watched this Mallorcan lad
in a match? No racket slamming, no pouting,
no yelling at the referee. Just sheer exuberance
in stroking backhand winners or racing to the net
to return an opponent's backspins. Simple joy!
Like my horse, Eagle, racing across the desert
in the morning with young Arthur in the saddle.

Like manifold pleasures along life's path
when we open ourselves to God:
The rivers clap their hands,
the mountains sing,
and the sea roars its applause.
Oh, God, in your presence is fullness of joy!

Psalm 16:11

A Maimed Pig

For some diet-deficient or malevolent reason,
the sow had chewed off one little piglet's hind legs.
"Papa," I begged, "don't kill it!"
So he spared the piglet and put me in charge.
I treated its wounds and fed the little creature.
For months before it finally became a hog
(and went to market), this pig would trail me
around the yard, dragging its maimed body,
grunting happily, and gobbling up goodies.
If such bonding can occur between a boy and a pig
how much more, and at a higher level, between persons!
Sometimes we're helpers, sometimes the helped ones,
sometimes the victim, sometimes the good Samaritan.
"Forasmuch as you did it unto one of the least of these,
declared Jesus, "you did it unto me."

Stubby the Jealous Cat

Stubby came as a bonus from a New Hampshire farmer
peddling maple syrup. We had purchased a gallon!
Stubby had lost his tail sometime, or had been docked,
and maybe for that reason had a bit of an attitude.
He became very possessive of his adopted family,
basking royally in the center of attention.
But when we brought our twin baby girls home,
King Stubby's imperial status plummeted.
His cozy empire had been invaded! In a fit of pique
he sulked behind the washing machine for days,
insulted that these noisy creatures took center stage.

When we left for Oregon some months later
we took the twins, of course,
but left Stubby behind. How true the proverb:
"Pride goes before destruction,
and a haughty spirit before a fall."
Sulking is more obvious in others than in oneself,
it seems, which is why the adage
rightly counsels a lowly spirit.

Ovine Beauty

Victoria was a beauty queen, winning purple ribbons
at state fairs and basking in well-preened glory.
Alas, she was barren. So, we sold her to a rancher
who claimed pampering prevents motherhood,
and that putting her out on the range to forage
with ordinary sheep would correct the situation.
Social leveling often proves beneficial, it seems,
but we never learned whether in Vickie's case
it achieved the expected fecundity.

Sweet-spirited Elizabeth (Becky), on the other hand,
too angular to win purple, bore lambs beautifully
and won ribbons for being a wonderful mother.
"Charm is deceptive, and beauty is fleeting,"
reads an old proverb, "but a woman who fears
the Lord is to be praised."
Now that perfume and other beautification aids
are hyped by ads showing slightly hirsute males
glaring at us, we can turn that adage gender neutral.

God's approval is what counts, not that of culture gurus.
This sure is good news for us ordinary people,
and a warning to fawned-over folks not to act uppity.
The old sage Samuel put it succinctly:
"People look at the outward appearance,
but the Lord looks at the heart."

Proverbs 31:30; 1 Samuel 16:7

A Pony Named Sue

We once had a pony named Sue. We paid $300 for her,
with a proviso that her next colt would go to the seller.
Fair enough for owning a horse our children could enjoy,
we thought. Unlike my childhood horse, Eagle, however,
Sue didn't like to be ridden. In fact, if we rode her
around trees we had to keep a tight rein
lest she veer under branches to sweep us off her back!
Her coat was dirty white in color and so was her heart.
The children gave up on her and rode their bikes instead.

So I rode Sue occasionally. She about knocked my head off
one day when I wasn't vigilant. Angrily, I kicked her
in the ribs, yanked the reins hard, and yelled at her.
Well, the time came for her to deliver her foal.
She struggled, and finally I helped deliver the foal.
I recall even now the look of gratitude in her eyes.

Returning good for evil goes a long way
toward correcting orneriness,
both in the rider and the ridden.
We sold Sue soon after the colt was weaned.
I hope redemptive love continued to work
the meanness out of her, as it had out of me.

Charlie and Missy

Charlie and Missy were companionable. On a sunny day, Missy, the cat, used to rub up against her dog friend in loving ways mutually appreciated. Cross-cultural friendship extended to their human friends too. Of an evening, Missy would curl up in our laps and purr happily, kneading us gently with her paws. When old Missy died we grieved along with Charlie dog.

Charlie would wait patiently for us at the post office door, wagging his tail happily at neighbors who patted his head. He liked it that we let him engage in rapturous sniffing on an ambling oceanside walk to and from home, and was wont to lick our faces in appreciation.

Like the lilies of the field our animal friends didn't worry about tomorrow, they didn't fret. They sopped up affection easily, reciprocated it readily. No strings attached, no keeping score, no pettiness. Charlie and Missy shared the joy of living with each other and with their human friends. They demonstrated what Jesus taught and Paul wrote: "Love is patient, love is kind." Like Charlie and Missy we can reach across boundaries to enjoy one another in the sunshine of God's love.

In Memory of Duffy

We miss hearing your happy purr.
We miss feeling your soft fur
against our faces.
We are sad at empty spaces
in our day, but oh, so glad
you came our way!
For God's creatures great and small
we thank him for you, now,
most of all.

Quarrelsome Hog

A teenage girl at a county fair was demonstrating her hog, a young boar. Anyone raised on a farm knows how difficult it is to make pigs do anything, let alone parade in a circle. (My father cleverly exploited porcine stubbornness; to load hogs into a trailer he'd put a bucket over their heads and let them back themselves up the ramp!)

Well, this girl's hog squealed and lashed out at competitors and their exhibitors. Only the assistance of a stout attendant interposing a plywood shield prevented the broken circle from becoming utter chaos. The shield didn't hurt the hog, but protected it—as well as others—from getting injured. To have a shield handy is prudent in any circle.

Sheep Dog Trials

See how eagerly they obey the shepherd's voice,
racing to fetch sheep from a distant field,
to bring them through designated gates, and,
within time limits, into a pen, upon which
the master shuts the gate, enfolding the flock.

If the master calls, "lay by!" they crouch down to avoid
frightening the sheep. "Away" and "come-by" tell them
to circle the flock. "Get back!" settles spooked ones.
How well they've learned shepherding nuances:

"stand," "take time," "lie down," "slow down," "in here,"
"walk up," "that'll do!" Occasionally a rebel bolts
from the others and must be brought back
oh, so patiently, without scattering the flock.

May I as adeptly heed the Master's voice!

Gertrude and Joe

Gertrude and Joe build a nest on a neighbor's roof
and each year raise a nestling there. How patiently
this seagull couple together feed, protect,
and nurture each year's fuzzy bundle of feathers,
and in a few months teach it to fly off the roof
out onto the rocky shore. Sometimes older siblings
fly back home to visit, to pester mama for food,
and to check out the latest family addition.
We like to check out this family also.

"One generation commends your works to another;
they tell of your mighty acts," wrote the psalmist.
Human nestlings need patient nurture too.
Each year little ones enter our families,
our communities, our churches, our world.
Gertrude and Joe remind us how important it is
to nurture the "next generation" in love and truth,
so as young adults they can "fly off the roof"
and cope wisely on our world's rocky shores.

Psalm 145

The Crows of Yachats

We took a special liking to the crows that lived
in our Yachats neighborhood. Crows are smart.
Every now and then we'd hear a particular call
and crows would swoop in from all corners
of the neighborhood to rout out an intruder or
to protect their nestlings. In coordinated attack
they would dive-bomb hawks who ventured
into their territory, hassling the stronger birds
until they left to hunt elsewhere.

Fern started feeding the crows, putting cat food
under a shore pine tree near a fence in our yard.
At first the crows whooped it up, calling all family
and friends to the feast. But that attracted
the stronger seagulls who promptly muscled in
and gobbled up the treats. So the crows learned
to be quiet in their signals, to use their eyes,
to be discreet, not to "crow" about their luck.
Sometimes of a morning one would perch upon the sill
and peek into our kitchen window to see if breakfast
was on the way, and softly caw to us if it wasn't.
There's something to be said for community,
for strength in numbers, but even more
for cooperation and common sense.

Green Pastures

Just outside historic Lafayette, Oregon, is a dairy farm. One can see scores of cows walking from barn to pasture, grazing, or resting. From the road one must look for them, because sometimes they're in one pasture, sometimes in another of several fenced acreages. The farmer rotates these pastures and irrigates them in timely fashion. Never overgrazed, the grass stays green and luscious. Thanks, farmer friend, for providing good pastures!

If I were a cow I'd like this farmer. As a human being I'm glad our heavenly Father keeps us well nourished and cared for in places (and times) where he leads us. Sometimes, unlike Lafayette cows, we resist changing from one venue to another. Accepting divine guidance, however, brings contentment: peace with ourselves, our neighbors, and the world. As the psalmist said, God makes us "to lie down in green pastures."

Psalm 23 KJV

Sonnet to a Greedy Squirrel

A squirrel lives in a redwood tree
enjoying seeds we liked to place
each early morning at its base.
Squirrel is greedy as can be.
When neighbors came to feed, you see
he selfishly began to chase
the two away from seeds at base
of what he claims to be his tree.

In separate piles we put the seed,
easier thus for all to share—
a sign we hoped that he might heed—
alas, he didn't give a care.

Gifts unshared each day
God may take away.

Tributes to Friends

Twin Oaks

For many years these twin oaks
accommodated their foliage
to surrounding flora,
variegated by tides of time.

Now they stand symmetrically
above well-tended fields
and cast a silhouette of love
against a softening sky.

to Jim and Elizabeth Bishop
June 15, 1986

Fifty is Nifty

Fifty is nifty—
it's nicer than thirty
(although not so flirty),
and better than twenty
(with uncertainties many),
and much more fun than
when you were ten.

to Ellouise Chandler
June 6, 1987

Home Economics Teacher

My friends, I give tribute,
I give well-deserved praise
to this home economics teacher,
who with grace and goodwill
cuts fine fabric carefully
and fashions it fittingly
to human need—ever
with an eye to style
as well as to utility—
doing work that is neat,
pleasing, and professional.

Yes, my friends,
I give high praise
to a George Fox College
home economics teacher.
Her name is Helen Street.

1987

The World Has Changed

The world has changed
since you were born.
Heavenly sparkles dance in the rain,
winds exuberantly
sweep the sea
to freshen the atmosphere,
and the joyous sun warmly
embraces the waiting earth.

Our world has changed
since you were born.
Waiting is worth the wonder of life,
our son, our son!
Rain, wind, sun, earth,
these join with God, kin,
neighbors, and us
to celebrate your birth.

Our world has changed
since you were born.

to Matthew, born to Phil and Karen Schuster
1989

To a Scholar

I give tribute to a scholar,
more than to a bridge.
Generally we take both for granted.
Ponder pilings driven into bedrock,
mind multi-stranded cables
that bear steel and concrete
pathways over river, bog
and estuary. Feel the bridge
flex but hold against the wind,
faithful to divine law,
to architectural dreams,
and to much skilled labor.
Imagine the harmonics
required to handle stress
and strain of truth.
Appreciate burdens posed
by sloth's subsidence
and by deceit's erosion
along the human road
from ignorance
to knowledge.
Celebrate with me the scholar
who offers access to the world,
turning the ear to wisdom
and the heart to understanding—
a bridge of truth for generations.
I give tribute to a scholar,
more than to a bridge.

to William Green
April 17, 1989

Anniversary

On this anniversary day
past catches up with present,
and laying hand to arm
says "Why don't we stop
a bit and decide what
to take into the future."
"Sure!" now replies to then.
So they find a place to rest
in the autumn shade
of the tree of life,
surrounded by azure sky
and sounds of crashing surf.
They agree to throw out
regret at roads not taken,
rancor over various rebuffs,
false guilt over misfortune,
a tangle of remorse over
failures long-forgiven, and
assorted worn-out anxieties.
With the load thus lightened
present and past shoulder
again their cherished burdens
within sweet joys of conjugal love:
work routines, ministry, worship,
friendships, thoughtful children,
eager grandchildren. And then
they stride into the future together.

to Harlow and Gertrude Ankeny
September 8, 1989

Habitat for the Spirit

Their years of Christian ministry
lie not behind but around them.
These years surround all for whom
the present has included—
a habitat for the Holy Spirit
landscaped by the minds
and hands of faithful stewards.

This habitat for the Holy Spirit
offers faith exciting as shadowed
mountains—magnificent, scary,
a realm to be lost and found in—
a wondrous land where things
old and new, small and large
are seen through Jesus' eyes.

This habitat for the Holy Spirit
offers hope strong as headlands
uplifted between soil and sea,
fog-bound at times, or lashed by wind.
But then again in splendor prismed
by a sinking sun, a questing place
for persons wanting truth and God.

This habitat for the Holy Spirit
offers love tenacious as the sea,
billowing, crashing, even terrifying:
a place mysterious, all embracing,
old as time, young as tomorrow—
life's Alpha and Omega, its horizon
an invitation and a benediction.

to Frank and Jean Cothrell
1990

Love in Sunday School

The Bible lesson is about Hosea,
whose efforts to restore
a fickle and unfaithful wife
constitute a parable
of God's unconditional love.
We discuss the implications
of covenant for Israel,
its meaning for the Church.

But the best commentary on love,
God's, and ours, that Sunday
is demonstrated convincingly
by a loving senior disciple
who continuously caresses his
faithful but incapacitated wife.

to Laurence and Rosa Skene

1992

first published in
The Sacred Ordinary

The Historian

Historian, traveler in time,
custodian of the maps,
cartographer of the centuries,
you know where we've been;
tell us where we are going.
We need better directions
and fewer diversions
from life's course now,
for the day of the Lord
has broken upon us
bringing heavy weather,
and we must break camp.

Help us regain our bearings.
How do we skirt the lake
that has become a swamp?
Which are the surest paths
into an unknown future?
We would climb the pass
to discover better worlds;
but the peaks are obscured
from our view. Surely
you have seen the peaks,
historian, traveler in time.
Let your wisdom guide us.

to Lee Nash
1992

In the Radiant Circle

These fifty years are not gone;
they are not over and past.
They shape the meaning of today.
Daily these years swirl around
like breezes pleasant to the face,
like music soft to the ear.
The years retain their force
like the aroma of mown hay,
and the taste of good food.
Time can be cumulative.

To the eyes of a man and woman
who love each other and God
more now than ever before,
each sunrise compounds glory,
each sunset prisms bright hope
that carries through the night.
Their family reflects this light.
Friends and other beneficiaries
also bask in the radiant circle
of their golden years.

in tribute to Mahlon and Hazel Macy
1992

Around the Emptiness

There is no way to fill the void
when a beloved daughter dies;
a section of the soul is bare.

But all around that emptiness
one can plant good memories.
These, when intermixed with seed
from the Spirit's gracious sowing,
will transform that torn-up place
into resurrection space.

To that garden, green and growing,
many will come, drawn by a need
for the faith, the love, the care
they surely will discover there.

to Dan McCracken
September 12, 1993

To a Surgeon

You correct the consequences
of infirmity, misfortune,
and general foolishness,
patching up our bodies
and putting our minds at rest.
An arm of the Almighty
you are, skilled surgeon!

For this you are paid well,
although beneficiaries
of your ministry may not be
mindful of an accumulating
debt of time that you owe
to others: to your family,
to friends, to yourself.

Thank you for using your time
to extend ours, for expending
your body and your mind
to make us whole (or at least
healthier), for respecting
our dignity, and even sharing
the burden of our pain.

to Robert R. Poole
1993

Keeper of Records

Someone has to keep score
to make sure acquisition
of knowledge gets organized
into manageable units
of time, space, and energy.

Someone has to certify credits
in the marketplace of ideas
so that, quantitatively
at least, tuition and salaries
are accounted for.

Someone must hold, transcriptable,
the record of truth sought,
and how diligently,
so that integrity marks
both student and scholar.

That someone, gatekeeper
at the door of wisdom,
is our faithful registrar.
Thank you, Hector Munn,
for a job well done!

April 8, 1994

Sprightly at Ninety

Cheers and good wishes,
to friend Walter P. Lee,
as hale and sprightly
at ninety as ever can be
when lived in the power
and joy of the Lord.
Not grumpy, not bored,
not morose, not complaining,
whether it's sunny or raining.
So gracious and cheerful is he
that we always feel better
just talking with him.
Sometimes, we recall, how
his cautious "well, now!"
checked ill-advised schemes;
more often his words, so it seems,
showed doors, not hitherto seen,
that opened truth to our view.
Does Christ speak to the world
anymore? Can the church cope?
"Sure, God's mercies are new
every morning," says Walter P. Lee,
voice ringing with steadfast hope,
"we're walking the kingdom road!"

1994

Among Inuit and Aymara

From arctic Alaska,
south to Cordillera Real,
among Inuit and Aymara—
their name is blessed; prayers
ascend to God in praise
for ministry well tendered.

Worthily they wear Christ's name,
for they have borne the Cross;
they understand suffering love.
They know how dark despair
by faith is transformed
into bright kingdom hope!

They have partaken
of the bread of life.
The Spirit whispers to them
of resurrection promises.
This their family affirms,
as do their many friends.

to Earl and Janice Perisho
1994

A Good Wind

Each day dawns fresh as dew
upon this pair whom love binds
close together. Each evening, too,
displays the treasure that one finds
in ordinary places marked by
earthly sparkles of God's glory.
Can such tranquility defy
life's pain, its losses, the sorry
state of things gone wrong?
Yes! Oh yes! For hope is strong;
faith finds wonder everywhere
journeying from here to there.

Their memory compass will not fail;
a Good Wind has filled the sail.

to George and Elenita Bales
June 25, 1994

That's Stan!

Wisdom enhanced by wit—
well, *usually* enhanced.
Biblical expositions honed
to sharp, prophetic truths
by discernment about what
is happening in our world.
Sermons sparkling from
narrative gems cut
with ironic facets.

That's Stan!

Laughter that lightens
the burdens we share
in conversation, and signals
a gentle and loving pastor
who accepts us as we are,
who cares more about
who we can become
through Christ's power
than about who we were.

That's Stan!

to Stan Thornburg
1996

At the Spirit's Nudging

"Sing to the Lord a new song," urged the psalmist.
At the Spirit's nudging Inez responded gladly:
"With organ and piano I can help others do that!"
So every Sunday for years Yachats worshipers
prayed during her organ preludes and offertories,
sang hymns to piano accompaniment, and breathed
(or shouted) "amen" as the choir joyfully celebrated
the wonder of redemption and new life in Christ.

"With trumpets and the sound of the horn
make a joyful noise before the King, the Lord,"
urged the psalmist. At the Spirit's nudging
Frank said, "Sure, this is something I can do!"
So he gathered like-minded friends and together
they made joyful noise, skillfully, loudly,
melodically on many community occasions,
on all sorts of trumpets and horns—and drums.

"With gratitude in your hearts sing psalms,
hymns, and spiritual songs to God," urged Paul.
Gratitude to God includes our thanks to you.
God bless you in your new home!

to Frank and Inez Lutz
Psalm 149:1 TNIV; Psalm 98:6 ESV; Colossians 3:16 NRSV

Thank You!

Someone has to make sure water
flows cleanly from Reedy Creek
to faucets so we can quench our thirsts,
cook our cereal, wash our clothes,
and enjoy hot showers.

Someone must insure that sewage
reaches the ocean environmentally
okay, to look after streets and facilities,
and to answer citizen questions
about ordinances and permits.

Someone has to find solutions
to vexing infrastructure problems
and to implement solutions efficiently,
keeping city council so well informed
they make good decisions.

Someone must supervise employees,
handle contracts and budgets,
and do so pleasantly and effectively.
For twenty years that someone has been you.
God used you to serve others.

Thank you!

to Rod Carrasco
2001

A Steady Beacon

Like the strong flood light
beaming seaward from your roof
night after night, your life, dear friend,
has been a steady beacon guiding us
through calm or stormy circumstance.
Your bright confidence in Christ,
sparkling through your winsome smile,
has taught us clearly that God cares.

Your decades' worth of thoughtful love
has demonstrated that the earth
indeed can be a pleasant place,
that serenity can conquer stress,
that joy can crown simple duties
quietly done in Jesus' name,
that love for family, neighbors,
strangers, can heap up eternal gain.

Louise, the Light that lit your passing
shines into the shadows of our hearts.
Now death seems less scary
and heaven more real, and closer,
because you are there.

Louise Hanson
November 6, 1997

Settings

Goldsmiths and silversmiths skillfully fashion
settings for precious metals extracted,
refined, and carefully crafted from ore
dredged from the earth and from the sea
by the labors of many persons.

Similarly our printer friend
skillfully fashions into settings
language crafted from raw thought,
patiently drawn from the human spirit
by the labor of many persons.

The Word made flesh is thus proclaimed
in truths profound as all creation:
heart to heart, mind to mind.
What artistry—to craft from print
settings for the Light Divine!

to Dick Eichenberger
December 30, 1997

Goodbye, Ed

We will miss you, Ed.
We will miss your firm handshake
and your soft and loving eyes.
We will miss your creative mind—
even your lunchtime repartee.
We will miss your commanding
but servant presence at George Fox.

Most of all we will miss
your cheerful witness to Christ
when our faith faltered.
One day we'll join you, Ed.
Meanwhile explore and enjoy
the beautiful new campus
of God's eternal kingdom.

to Ed Stevens
May 21, 1998

The Logic of Your Love

Thank you for living
so joyously among us.
You taught us much:
to overcome losses
triumphantly,
to find adventures
in contentment,
to enjoy being on stage
or in the audience,
to have fun with family
and with friends.

A cheerful spirit,
beautifully Christlike,
was your finest healing art.
Under the logic of your love
even jumbled up things
came together, somehow,
and made sense.

to Alice Ross
July 7, 1998

We Belong Together!

By calendar time fifty years
have passed since that hot
summer day in Iowa
when ceremoniously
and prayerfully, before
family and friends, we pledged
our love in formal words
already whispered lovingly:
"We belong together!"

We still belong together.
Our love has been tested
by adversity and success,
strengthened by children
and grandchildren, sustained
by sturdy friendships,
and undergirded by wisdom
gained in serving others.

Best of all, God is with us;
and though memories enrich
the present, hope in Christ
guides our future together.

to Wayne and Berthamay Roberts
July 26, 1998

Such Enduring Love

A sixty-nine year romance
can't be measured easily,
like teaspoons to the cup,
or by counting tree rings.
These ways can never tally up
the good things life brings
when love prevails faithfully
through time and circumstance.

Life together, now and tomorrow,
is measured rather by the beauty
of love that, sunlike, bestows
its rays wherever human needs
arise. Such enduring love shows
itself in thoughtful deeds
to others and by civic duty—
and triumphs over sorrow.

to Charlie and Louise Canfield

1998

Blue Ribbon, 2005
Retirement Communities Poet Fest
Eugene, Oregon

Poems using similar metaphors
were sent to Hoffy and Leona Drahn,
George and Dorothy Thomas,
and Dea and Lois Cox.

At the Border

So, friend Don,
you've reached the border
of the promised land
and soon may enter.
Friend, your radiant, joyous
faith in Christ
these past few years
has enriched our lives.
And so we wave goodbye
in resurrection hope
that we will meet again—
across the border.

to Don Leavett
1998

It's Jolly Fun

Who can predict the path love takes,
spanning distances of time and space
to bring together one woman
and one man to share the rest
of life's journey hand in hand
(not apart), heart with heart?

Forecasting such a circumstance—
whether fate, a happenstance,
or benign divine conspiracy—
is difficult; but celebrating
that serendipitous event
is not. In fact it's jolly fun.

to Vail and Izzy Palmer
January 31, 1999

Sonnet to Grace

Here's a toast to Gracie Prest.
Let's celebrate her hundred years
with laughter, happiness—no tears—
for by her life we've all been blessed.

Hear it again for Gracie Prest!
Loving mother soothing fears,
friendships never in arrears.
She has passed life's hardest tests.

What does her century signify?
It signals struggle, sorrow, pain,
such things no one can deny.
But Gracie ever and again

cheerfully, faithfully, trod
that golden path to God.

June 9, 2001

To Blossom Beautifully

Unseen in common soil,
seeds find a godly power
hour by hour to grow,
to thrive, and eventually
to flower fragrantly
under conditions varying
from blazing sun
to drenching rain.

So it is with marriage.
A man and woman together,
with God's grace, find the space
to grow and prosper,
year by year,
through all sorts of weather,
and after half a century
still blossom beautifully.

Russ and Barb Ferrell

2002

*similar poems used for
other anniversary occasions*

So Fully Whole

To reach the age of ninety years
and to remain so fully whole
in body and in mind and soul
through joyous times,
and even tears,
is an event to celebrate!

It is not just genetic wealth
that explains your vibrancy,
but a certain godly clarity
of purpose
that has fostered health,
and enables us to celebrate!

Happy birthday, Lewis!

to Lewis Hoskins
2004

A Birthday Prayer

Lord, I thank you for Chase,
for his passion to learn and to serve,
for orderliness in mind and body,
for his joyous Christian faith,
for intergenerational friendships.

Open his mind to all truth.
Shield him from subtle sins,
especially from self-deception.
Nurture his latent gift for words
spoken, written, incarnated.

Surround him with companions
on faith's often arduous climb.
Correct him when he's wrong,
affirm him when he's right.
Love him all the time.

Hear my prayer, Lord,
for my young friend, Chase.

for Chase Willcuts
2005

Tributes to Family

Bottom Line

Debit side:

At age seventy-five
one isn't as agile
as at fifty-five;
bones are more fragile
than at thirty-five.

Credit side:

At age seventy-five
one isn't as worried
as at twenty-five,
and not so hurried,
as at forty-five.

Bottom line:

Since age sixty-five
a greater freedom
keeps memories alive,
and adds much wisdom
to the year seventy-five.

to Ivan Adams
1989

Six Bits

You are now seventy-five,
six bits of a dollar. Man alive,
you're fifteen past three score,
and headed toward more!
The years have not gone away,
but are just clustered around
you in memories that stay
close by, in sight and sound,
in smell, taste, and touch,
through your work and play,
and in friendships and such.
Memories near as today—
memories dear as love
lit from Above.

to brother Warren
1995

To Warren

Congratulations on your birthday!
Can it really be the great eight-oh?
Celebrating eighty is a way
to honor a life that means so
much to us. What more to say?
This word, cherished brother; blow
the candles toward, let's say,
another decade, or two. Flow
with the tide of life. Hey!

July 18, 2000

A Good Story

Each day dawns fresh as dew
that silvers alfalfa fields
for these two whom love binds
together. Each sunset yields
shared contemplations that renew
joy in earthy tasks. They find
golden sparkles of God's glory
in things exotic or mundane.
Can tranquility defy life's pain,
triumph over things gone wrong?
Yes! Oh yes! For hope is strong
and faith finds God everywhere,
journeying from here to there.
Fifty years is a good story.

to Warren and Lora Roberts
1997

In Festive Ways

In festive ways we celebrate
each passing year and contemplate
its meanings for us. Life is more
than numbers, more than keeping score.

Your birthday is a special date
for brothers, too, a time to wait
in silence until love restores
kinship feelings as before.

In that stillness I recall
contentment in our family life.
I remember, most of all,
loving care instead of strife.
I feel your care again;
I feel it once again.

to sister Lucille Adams

A Clarity of Purpose

To reach the age of eighty years
and to remain so fully whole
in body and in mind and soul
through times of joy and times of tears
is an event to celebrate!

Does luck or does genetic fate
explain to us your vibrancy?
Or, instead, is it a wealth
of character that fosters health?
I believe it is a clarity

of godly purpose, and not fate,
that confers longevity.
You have learned to be content,
to discern through what is sent
how one can find serenity.

So, Lucille, let's celebrate!

to sister Lucille
1997

The Year Fifty

The year fifty is numerically round,
a word that sounds much neater
than saying "half century."

This year fifty means much more.
It opens a door to memory's hall
full of treasures that offer joy:
good times and hard times,
baby events, childhood things,
and what adolescence brings.
Now we cherish adult relationships.
But mostly, son, we remember love.

Yesterday and tomorrow converge today,
Beyond remorse or sorrow about
what might have been is joy:
joy in the grace of God,
delight in family and friends,
pleasure in work and play.

Let joy mark the day!
Happy fiftieth, Lloyd!

1996

Merits Silver

Twenty-five years
of marriage merits silver:
for constancy of love,
for integrity to truth—
tested by pressures
to force apart
what God has joined
together.

Twenty-five years
of marriage merits silver:
for a loving, loyal family,
for adventures shared
happily, and for troubles
faced, and mistakes
resolved, squarely
and together.

Twenty-five years
of marriage merits silver:
for skilled teaching,
for an exemplary use
of talents and time
to serve humanity,
especially children,
together.

to Teri and John Rogers
March 29, 2000

To Trish

When you were a child I likened you
to a graceful deer, poised between
curiosity and caution. Trish, you remain
eager to experience life. You're cautious,
though. Having experienced pain
God has taught you about grace,
about the freedom of forgiving love,
about compassion for all creatures,
human or otherwise, including
an assortment of cats who
show up at your door.
Like your friends and family
they know a kind person
when they see one!

2007

To Teri

When you were a child I likened you
to a bright stream with laughing ripples
and smiling sand. Teri, you still draw
people gladly to your shores:
loved ones, friends, associates,
school children and their parents,
even wandering strangers.
They all find peace and happiness
within your warm personal space,
attracted by what they rightly
perceive as radiant and inviting.
Your love, sunlit by God's grace,
keeps on rippling down the years,
to quiet fears and heighten joys!

2007

A.O.R.

Under the sky of southern Idaho
was where he first drew breath.
A pioneer's son, with an artist's soul
began exploring his life's depth.

Plow and trace and singletree,
replaced by curiosity,
guiding this seeker's path toward
his vision of the Lord.

Thought, words, and dialogue,
challenged and tested truths,
of what is man and who is God
and what defines man's worth.

Arthur: Dad, Papa, and friend,
scholar, minister, and leader lends
clarity and wisdom
in telling of God's love.

Happy Birthday, Dad, Grandpa

by Teri, John, and John David
January 7, 2001

Tributes to Fern

Most of All

I loved you in our spring of life
when passions blossomed forth
like eager yellow daffodils.

I loved you in those summer days
when work flowed everywhere
like sun's green mark upon the hills.

I'll love you in the winter, too,
when rest like snow upon red roots
anticipates spring call.

But now I love you most of all—
when yellow, green, and red
blend in to fall.

December 17, 1980

first published in Sunrise and Shadow

To Fern

I like to watch the waves with you
and monitor the tides.
Sometimes the sea, before our view,
is calm, at other times in storm.
Within our sea of love abides,
also, such rich variety,
such freedom, in Eternal form.

1982

Birthday

Look around you,
sweetheart.
The landscape glows
from the beauty
of your touch,
and the horizon
promises a future
already nurtured
by your love.

1984

And Wait for More

Three score and ten,
and once again
we celebrate
the special day
and wait
for more—

Four score, then,
or more—it depends;
but soon or late
we know the way
is but a gate;
there's more in store.

Therefore we send
love once again,
happy to relate
life's joys, and say
to all, celebrate
life forevermore.

1983

Each Passing Year

Each passing year
binds our love
closer to a rhythm
joyously Divine.
Sun follows rain,
storms yield
to tranquility,
earth kisses sky.

Tides ebb and flow,
sometimes softly,
sometimes loudly.
Time frames eternity
with days that go
down to sunset fire
and nights that rise
to soft starlight.

And like light,
our love triumphs
over dark!

1989

published in Drawn by the Light

Am I the Same?

Am I the same brash sophomore
who asked you for a date
one day so long ago?
The answer: yes and no.

Sometimes now, as then, I wait,
anxious, hoping for
assent to my request
on one thing or another.

But I'm a different person, too,
knowing how much more
your love reciprocates
the love I hold for you.

1993

Golden Wedding

Fifty years for you,
and fifty years for me,
along time's highway,
add up to a century
of life together.

But if we count meandering
along detours of ignorance,
delving into caves of sorrow,
and soaring flights of ecstasy,
why then the time is much longer.

And if we put memories, hopes,
present joys, family, and God
into the manifold calculation
of time spent, it becomes
an eternity together.

1993

Dorchester

The Dorchester House is now
a retirement home, but observing
its continued, charming ambience
brings memories of our honeymoon
there fifty-three years ago,
at Oregon's finest beach resort.
You were my sweetheart then, Fern.
You are so now, gracious, charming.
I love you!

1996

By Sun-filled Hopes

I loved you in the spring of life
when things were green and growing.
I loved you in our summer, too,
in labors warm and sometimes wearing.
I loved you in the pleasant fall of life,
amid a cumulus of tasks completed.
Anticipating wintertime, I love you
when darkening days are lightened
by sun-filled hopes for love eternal.

2000

More Synchronously

She turns out the lights
that he leaves on.
He shuts the doors
that she leaves open…
But they do many other things
much more synchronously.
Like sleeping contentedly
in the same bed, sharing work
and meals together, playing Scrabble
and golf in seasonal rhythm,
enjoying children, grandchildren,
great-grandchildren, friends,
neighbors, animals,
and a hundred fascinating places.

Praying with hands and hearts
interlaced and uplifted,
and together worshiping the One
before whom they promised
always to love and cherish
each other. Which they have done
reasonably well, thanks to health
and the nudging of divine grace,
for many good years.

Now, with sixty years together,
the nudgings of divine grace
are even more empowering
for the years ahead.

2003

Morning Prayer #1

Each morning is a gift to us from heaven.
For this gift we praise you, Lord!
At the dawning of the light we waken
to the sound of crashing surf
and to the sight of seagulls soaring.
Ritually, we turn to each other.
I open my arms. You lay your head
on my shoulder; our legs entwine.
Our bodies get comfortable.
So do our minds and hearts.
Half awake, half dreaming,
we caress each other, basking
in the light of sixty years together,
loving, working, sharing, caring.
And when on that Great Morning
You awaken us to resurrection
sights and sounds, Lord,
we will be ready.

November 7, 2003

Milepost 62

At milepost 62, my dear,
we're cruising happily together
in bright as well as stormy weather.
And while it's not yet fully clear
how many mileposts still remain,
before we reach that golden shore
(we hope there will be many more),
one thing that surely will sustain
our trip, as heretofore, is love
a passion fueled from Above.
Fern, let's relax awhile,
enjoy each blessed mile!

2005

Morning Prayer # 2

Each morning is a gift from heaven
for which we thank you, Lord!
At dawning of the day we waken
to sounds of trucks fetching food
for us Friendsview folks, yes, but
also to a sight of clouds scudding
across the sky to frame the trees
nearby and on Chehalem's mountain!
Ritually we turn to each other,
I open my arms and you, sweet Fern,
lay your head on my shoulder,
and, half awake, half dreaming,
we caress each other, basking in
sixty-three joyous years together.
And when on that Bright Morning,
Lord, you awaken us into glory,
we'll be ready, hands and hearts
clasped, and in your arms!

November 7, 2006

Tributes to Grandchildren and Great-grandchildren

Robin

Like the morning sun
Robin brightens the sky,
offering verdant promises
to shadowed earth.

Her rays illumine
the world honestly,
but with gentle warmth
and bright hopes.

Storms and darkness
may obscure this light,
but not its power—
Cross-tested love.

1989

Upon Turning Thirty-six

Robin, at thirty-six (as at your birth)
you continue to brighten our days
like a warm sun after weeks of rain.
Through thoughtful words and deeds,
bright smiles, hugs, good conversation—
reflecting a strong marriage and
wise and gentle parenting—
you continue, sweet Robin Louise,
to be for your grandparents,
and for many other people,
God's messenger of love.

2007

April

April is a mountain stream
tumbling in torrents
from source to salted sea,
feeding a thirsty land.

Sometimes she bounces noisily
among the scattered rocks,
or tests her strength
against a stubborn shore.

But often she tiptoes quietly
because God says, "Shh!
Don't frighten the rabbits
and our other meadow friends."

1989

April at Thirty

April is a mountain stream surging
spring-fed from the Almighty,
tumbling and rippling joyously.
She nourishes a thirsty land
in whatever human terrain
her love flows through,
sweeping away storm debris
and rubbish all the way
from source to purifying sea.

2007

Seth

Seth is a young fir tree
reaching for the light,
boughs flexing with the wind,
needles glistening in the rain.

Although at home, well-rooted
upon the forest floor,
at times he stands alone
and searches out the sky.

And God who made that sky
is reaching out to him
to celebrate the double search
in joy—gift and Giver!

1989

Seth

Seth is a strong young fir tree
branches reaching heavenward,
boughs flexing in the winds
as he weathers life's storms.
A friendly, diligent worker,
he radiates goodwill to others—
coworkers, family, friends—
while growing in the sunlight
of God's beneficent grace.

2007

Heidi

Heidi is a warm spring sun
breaking (somewhat timidly)
through stormy clouds
after a rainy night.

Her spreading smile,
radiant from fire within,
removes a lingering chill
and lights the room with love.

And when her eyes
reach up to embrace,
it's like God's rainbow
caressing a broken world.

1989

Heidi at Thirty

Heidi spreads the sunshine
of her love to all around her,
family, friends, school children,
strangers on the street.
Amid the storms of life,
her smile, like a rainbow,
conveys God's promises
of good things to come,
to heal a broken world.

2007

Sarah

Sarah is a mountain meadow
fragrant with spring flowers;
storm clouds have fled away
and winter is forgotten.

The laughter of God,
flowing through her
thaws lingering snow banks
and softens the waiting soil.

Does the meadow nourish life?
As surely as pine candles
unfold their green needles
and reach for the April sun.

1989

Sarah

Sarah is a mountain meadow,
fragrant with flora, hospitable
to fauna, verdant with life.
Her cheerful spirit blesses
family and friends, and also
strangers passing through,
touched by her reflection
of the joyful, life-giving
love of God.

2007

John David

John David is a bright wave
jumping the rocks
and drenching the sand with joy
at the edge of a jubilant sea.

He empties his pockets
on the shore of our souls
at the surging of every tide—
agates, sea palms, shells—

earthly sparkles of heavenly glory,
accompanied by songs
from the rolling surf,
united in praise of God.

1989

John David

John David is a bright wave
surging now here, now there,
splashing with abandon
at the shores of our souls.
His surf tide sounds a rhythm
mysterious and haunting,
probing for a pattern
of meaning designed
by the Creator.

2007

Laura

Laura is an evening breeze
sweeping away cluttered air
and softening the bleak,
hot, and busy days.

She moves lightly over
languid streets and lazy trees
touching them with vibrancy
until they dance for joy.

Touching us with love
until we dance for joy
and the Spirit sweeps away
the clutter of our cares!

1989

Laura

Laura is a freshening breeze
that softens hot and busy days,
her own, and those of others.
Her vibrant energy,
guided by the Holy Spirit,
wafts down life's avenues,
stirring up creativity
in the use of things
for the good of all.

2007

Easter Baby

Aiden, Easter baby, April eleven—
blessedly you share a birth date,
not only with your mother,
but also, in the year of our Lord
(anno domini) two thousand four,
with the resurrected Christ.
Aiden, when each year we celebrate
your birthday we'll think of Jesus!
We'll be grateful for your parents
who brought you into this world
and for the risen Savior, too,
who offers all of us eternal life.
Aiden, sweet Easter baby,
God loves you! We do too!

2004

In Your Dark Eyes

Baby Quinn, in your dark eyes
I see pools of potentiality
glowing from inner fires
lately lit by the Almighty.

Through these bright eyes
you clutch mine, baby Quinn,
looking for love, for truth—
rekindling my own soul.

Whatever of truth and love
you find there, baby Quinn,
take it! All I ask in return
is one more bubbly smile.

2004

One of God's Gemstones

Mia Jade, you entered the world
eagerly looking and grasping,
letting us all know joyfully—
and very forthrightly—
that you've arrived and plan
to participate in it fully.
Oh, sweet baby, Mia Jade,
you're one of God's gemstones
waiting to be tumbled about
by life's gritty circumstances,
encompassed by family love,
and letting divine grace polish
you—body, mind, and spirit—
until you glow with godly fire.

2006

On Turning Seven

Zain, eager schoolboy,
you've now attained age seven;
and in four more short years,
not long, you'll be eleven!
Push aside all your fears.
So much is offered you:
numbers, words, and places,
many things to study and to do.
Learn well, my boy, and enjoy
truth discovered. From inner spaces
of your mind and heart, learn
to savor the wonderful world
that God has created.

2007

Tributes to Places

The Pleasant Ridge Schoolhouse

Close beside the road the schoolhouse rests,
elderly but dignified, spruced up
and waiting for children to sit on her lap
to learn mysteries of life and truth,
like generations before have done.

Sagebrush-grubbing pioneer children
learned arithmetic and spelling here;
they played hop-scotch and mumbly-peg,
and they climbed the catalpa tree.

Farm children who milked cows before breakfast
trudged here to learn geography, history,
and the names of state capitals.
At recess they played softball and marbles,
and ate wild onions to irritate the teachers.
And they climbed the catalpa tree.

Rural children who mowed lawns on Saturday
checked out library books to be read at home.
They raced at county track meets, played ball,
and at recess climbed the catalpa tree.

Then people got restless for the city.
Machines had subdued the land,
leveled it, and bent it to productivity.
Fewer brains and muscles were required
on the Ridge then, and families aged.
So the sons of the sons of the pioneers,
seeking better jobs, moved to cities

with new school buildings offering
closely-graded classes, music, art, sports,
and special-education programs—
all within efficient taxing districts.

Then the schoolhouse waited silently.
Children no longer kicked cans
on the dusty road en route to school,
no longer shouted and skipped and ran,
or wrote lessons in notebooks, or carved desks.
Blackboards then hung clean but cracked,
frames emptied of elemental but promising art.
And nobody climbed the catalpa tree.

The Pleasant Ridge School might have died,
except that thoughtful people intervened
and found the schoolhouse a job again.
Migrant children, whose parents toil
on land the pioneers tamed,
now learn mysteries of life and truth,
like generations before have done.
These have begun the exciting journey
of the mind. Where will it lead them
and their children, and grandchildren?
At recess these new pioneers shout and race,
and climb the old catalpa tree.
And a new generation of teachers exclaims,
oh, wisdom, how blessed are your children!

1990

I attended Pleasant Ridge School, near Caldwell, Idaho, 1928-1936.

Benediction

And so, O Lord,
we conclude
our litany of praise
and let the moment go.

Our lives have touched,
our energies
have merged
in common purpose.

Let us live henceforth
as better men and women
who will find ways
to unite again

hand in hand,
mind with mind,
to be good stewards
of your earth.

In Jesus' name,
Shalom!

dedication of Murdock Learning Resource Center
George Fox College
February 10, 1989

The Yachats Commons

Between still green hills
and a blue symphonic sea,
in the middle of a town
as pretty and friendly
as any you'll ever see,
is the Yachats Commons.

A gathering place
for writers and artists,
actors, crafters, dancers.

A learning, playing place
for children and other
curious persons of all ages.

A house that offers a grace
of enriched memories
for sturdy marchers in time
(veterans in life's race),
and scenarios of hope
for those at starting line.

A greensward album laced
by cords of public trust
for generations to read,
their pictures yet to paste.

A commons for lovers
of villages and habitats
built to last, not to waste.

A greensward to yield
peace to harried folk
who now enjoy nearby
trees, wetlands, open sky,
swings, and a ball field.

A park to walk in, or stroll,
or run, at fast or slower pace,
where picnics feed the body
and quiet talk the soul,
where spirit finds earth's face
and touches the Creator.

This is Yachats Commons.

September 1, 1990

Prayer for George Fox College

Lord God, today we celebrate a century
of education at George Fox College,
where truth revealed has been extolled.
Thank you for the wisdom that comes
through Scripture and the book of creation.
Thank you for the saving word
spoken into our hearts by Jesus Christ
and for the sanctifying Holy Spirit.
Lord God, receive our praise.

We have held truth's lamp so it could shine.
And in the world's eyes have succeeded.
But, Lord, do we find favor in your sight?
Give us courage to face uncertain futures.
Make us kingdom torchbearers.
In your providence, Almighty God,
grant us a good second century.
We pledge our faith; we will share
this covenant with those who follow.
Lord, light our way forward.

We pray for the Quakers now
and in the next century.
Grant discernment concerning
a legacy bequeathed by pioneers
who dreamed apostolic dreams.

May the Friends Church accept
the burden of George Fox College
conscientiously, as a sacred trust
for the Church and for the world.
Rekindle our fire, Lord.

We pray for those who give
their money to support the college,
now and in the next century.
They are co-heirs with Christ,
they are silent partners
with all who teach and learn.

Grant these givers joy in generosity.
Multiply their beneficence
like Galilee's shared bread and fish.
Bless gift and giver, Lord.

We pray for the trustees
now and in the next century.
Grant them a godly wisdom,
insightful as well as prudent,
to sustain an educational vision
over vagaries of time.
May trustees rightly set the course
during the second century
for George Fox College.
Grant them faithfulness, O God.

We pray for the administrators
now and in the next century.
Grant them understanding, patience,
and skills, so time and energy
expended on structures and systems
and resources, human or otherwise,
can sustain our stated mission
and release people to pursue truth
at George Fox College.
Uphold them by your Spirit, Lord.

We pray for the college staff
now and in the next century.
Theirs is the gift of helps.
They, too, gird themselves
to wash disciples' feet.
Quietly they labor day after day,
often within the shadow of others.
Renew their strength, give joy
to these companions of Jesus.
Bless them, Lord.

We pray for the faculty
now and in the next century.
Help them to handle knowledge
honestly. May they love students
as eagerly as they love truth.
Guard them against false pride.

May they make George Fox College
truly a school of prophets,
your voices in the present age.
Lord, be their master teacher.

We pray for students at George Fox
now and in the next century.
Open their minds and hearts for truth.
May their zest for life be guided
by a love for others, for the earth,
and for all its creatures. Give them
a vision for the peaceable kingdom,
and equip them to follow Jesus,
pioneer of the world's future.
Lord, keep them from idolatry.

We pray for the alumni
now and in the next century.
Guard their faith against erosion,
their hope against cynicism,
and their love against despair.
Keep before their eyes a vision
of what the world can be. May they
extend to others a helping hand
like ones that grasped them here.
Lord, bless George Fox College.

Centennial Convocation
1991

To Give You Hope and a Future

Celebrating a church centennial is like six,
actually, like *seven* exciting things.

ONE: finishing the first book of an exciting series.

TWO: feeling through your feet a throbbing power
as the odometer on your car turns 100,000 miles.

THREE: marching down the aisle at graduation
in solemn procession, a goal attained,
and wondering what will happen next.

FOUR: gliding past Mt. Hood on descent to Portland
after a long and wearisome plane ride,
reflecting upon what a beautiful
and useful world God has provided.

FIVE: reaching a peak after an exhilarating climb,
anticipating the next one just ahead higher
still, and those more distant
whose glistening horizons beckon
to greater effort, to greater glory.

SIX: preparing reports carefully
for a major company review,
certain that your work testifies
to skill and honest effort,
but anxious lest impartial scrutiny
reveals flawed stewardship.

SEVEN: finding treasure hid in a field
right where you live—so rich a find
you invest everything to secure it—
renewed in spirit by discovering
that God's realm is among us now,
finding incredible joy in knowing
that Jesus, the Christ, is present.

"The kingdom of heaven," said Jesus, "is like treasure hidden in a field. When a man found it, he hid it again, and then in his joy went and sold all he had and bought that field."

Reedwood Friends Church, Portland, Oregon
1993
Matthew 13:44-46

A New Beginning

Lord, we dedicate to You,
and to those we serve,
these new facilities.

Bless those who planned
the building and those
who constructed it.

This building represents
both a task completed
and a venture begun.

We dedicate the structure,
with its machines and tools;
we offer them to You.

May those who work here
reaffirm their calling
to effective publication.

Whether tasks be routine,
complicated, or creative,
frame their work with joy.

May the Media Commission
set wise goals and provide
dependable support.

May those who write
and those who read, together
honor Christ the Word.

Lord, let this new building
signify a new beginning
for Barclay Press.

Amen.

1994

Retirement Home

This retirement home is a great place
in many ways—good food, security,
health care, friends to visit with,
a hiking trail through the canyon,
pool tables and a workshop,
a golf course not far away,
campus activities across the street:
drama, musicals, ball games.

But one thing bothers me a bit:
all the old people, some of whom
were once my students!

The Little Log Church Museum

The little log church museum is a place
where present meets the past through artistry
and memorabilia, where the human race
(predictably and unpredictably)
exhibits all its foibles, hopes, and fears—
a mirror for the feelings we have known,
a sanctuary to ponder joy through tears.
Inwardly, not much different from our own,
the outward struggles of the pioneers
depicted here now feed the mind and soul.
And the artistry from Yachats peers
lets us see life joyously, and whole.

Yachats, Oregon

Jury Panel

As required, we arrive by 8:45 a.m.,
forty randomly selected citizens,
variable in vintage and in visage.
Soberly we file into a specified chamber
and sit quietly on wooden benches
so waxed they squeak if we wiggle.
After explaining court procedures
the clerk exits. Soon one person coughs,
then another, so I plop a lozenge
into my mouth. And we wait.

We sit silently for forty minutes,
shedding coats, squirming uneasily,
gazing at the seal of the state of Oregon,
pondering civic duties to a rhythm
of heels clop-clopping down the hall.
Is the case a civil or criminal one?
Will the attorney representing
the accused person befuddle us,
make us look dumb—or too smart—
for whatever reason, unacceptable?

The clerk enters the chamber again
and announces, "It may be a while,"
indicating that judge and litigants
aren't quite ready yet. "Relax," she says.
So we do. Some take bathroom breaks,
or stand up and stretch—find coffee.

The mood lightens. We begin to chat
with neighbors, renew acquaintances,
joke around, exchange pleasantries
about the recent freakish weather.

Then the hubbub gradually subsides.
The clock says 10:40. Novels reappear,
puzzles get finished. One man snores softly;
one woman knits peacefully. Finally
the clerk returns. "The accused," she says,
"has pled guilty and will be sentenced;
there will be no trial today.
You can all go home." So we leave,
to await another summons. Maybe.
They also serve who only *sit* and wait.

Tributes to Play

Scrabble Time

During evening Scrabble time
we mute the television 'til
the ten o'clock news comes on,
glancing now and then
at celebrities paraded across
the electronic Coliseum—
males fashionably stubble-chinned
and virally violent-looking—
females fashionably boob-uplifted
and suggestively sinuous,
and I wonder where the lions
are caged.

"Is it your turn, or mine"?

Golf for the Uninitiated

#1 Teeing Off

First, a word to non-golfers: Golf is not a flawed walk!
It's a game of skill played in places of natural beauty.
Like other sports, golf offers lessons for the spirit.

"Teeing off" refers to how one begins
each of the course segments ("holes")
varying in length from about 120 to 600 yards.
A tee is a tapered peg on which the golfer
places the ball for driving it with a "club."
Sports jargon calls this "addressing the ball."
This doesn't mean saying "hi," but positioning oneself,
taking practice swings, visualizing trajectory.
Then with feet planted correctly, arms firm,
shoulders relaxed, in a sweeping motion
one strikes the ball down the "fairway."

A golfer then goes to where the ball rests
and chooses another "wood" or "iron" to pitch
the ball upon a closely mowed grass circle,
dubbed a "green," and with a "putter" strokes
the little ball into a round hole: the "cup."
With mind and body in synch—long drives,
well-pitched approaches, and accurate putts—
yield intense aesthetic satisfaction!

"Teeing off" is important for daily beginnings, too.
Are body and mind relaxed and in synch?

Are eyes focused upon good, reachable goals
in respect to family, employment, friendships?
Are feet firmly planted in the truth?
Are shoulders flexible and arms strong?
If so, you're ready for life today!

#2 In the Rough

If all goes well, a golfer gets on the green after making one, two, or three strokes (depending upon whether it's a three-, four-, or five-par hole), and then sinks the ball into the cup in two putts. That's par. For most of us, golf—and life—doesn't go that smoothly. We muff shots, or hook or slice the ball into unmowed areas, into ditches or hillocks, or the ball bounces under branches or against a tree! That's called "landing in the rough."

Getting out of the rough really can be tough!
Extra strokes diminish fond hopes for par.
It takes boldness, confidence, and often luck
to thread the ball between tree trunks
or blast it from deep grass a significant distance.
Landing in the rough adds an element of adventure!
We try to stay on the fairway but if we don't, well,
it's a challenge to get out of trouble, at least cost.

Tough circumstances surround us. Sickness, accident, and economic adversity are hazards along life's course. As in the game of golf, we learn to extricate ourselves from situations arising from ineptitude or luck—it's how the ball bounces! Sometimes we cope easily but often spend extra time and energy to get out of the rough. Golfers soon learn that patience is preferable to rage. As the Bible says, "suffering brings patience."

#3 Bogies and Birdies

Is golf jargon still confusing? I'll explain.
You already know "par" means to match
the number of your swings to a standard
set by the course, three strokes for
a short hole, four for a medium sized one,
five for the long fairways. Well, "bogie"
means one over par, "double bogie": two,
"triple bogie": three...much more than that
you had better cool your temper—and/or
go practice on the driving range.

To "birdie" is to hole out one under par;
"eagle," two under par; and a "hole-in-one"
means your tee shot drops in the cup.
This doesn't happen often for amateur golfers.
(In sixty years of playing I've had only one.)
Actually, an eagle for a three-par hole
would be a hole-in one, wouldn't it?
Professionals and good amateurs find these
useful standards against which to pit
will and skill. They challenge strength
of mind and body and whet the appetite
for stimulating competition with one's peers.

#4 Out of Bounds

In golf, as in life, there are rules for acceptable conduct with penalties when violated. Golf courses are nestled among homes and other private properties, which are out of bounds. It isn't legitimate to play the ball from someone's lawn, even if you replace the "divot"! Penalty strokes are exacted for going out of bounds. Greens fees do not entitle you to play golf anywhere, just on the golf course. It's like life. There are boundaries: at home, at school, at work, on the road, in the community. Without boundaries social chaos ensues. Boundaries offer true freedom. The Ten Commandments state life's major moral boundaries, which Jesus summarized, to love God fully and to love your neighbor as yourself.

But there are minor boundaries too. You say, "excuse me," when inadvertently you jab someone with an elbow. You clean up what you've spilled. You apologize for inane remarks, or for being crabby with the family. Golfers don't deliberately drive a ball at joggers or folks working in nearby gardens. They have good intentions, but when performance doesn't rise to expectations they accept penalties for going out of bounds. And so should we, even given honorable intentions. Grace includes God's forgiveness for our bumbling, as well as for outright sinful conduct.

#5 Winter Rules

Sometimes a golf course itself is not up to par.
Rainwater has left puddles on parts of the fairway,
or winds have strewn limbs and leaves across it,
or turf has gotten torn up by service vehicles.
In such conditions golfers play under "winter rules"—
which permit "improving one's lie." Improving one's lie
does *not* mean fudging on position or score but rather
placing the ball on a nearby spot to make it playable.
Professional golf occurs on carefully tended courses
where deficiencies seldom arises or are quickly corrected.
If they do arise there are remedial rules so complex
"Pharisaic" is hardly strong enough to describe them.
But we amateur "duffers" play on public courses
which make allowances for bad course conditions,
allowing a player to improve the lie of the ball.
The trick is being honorable enough to accept
but not abuse such "situation grace," whether
on the golf course, on the job, or at home.
We often experience circumstances not fully ideal.
Disaster floods the fairways of our lives.
Storms cover our yards and minds with muck.
Evil traffic tears up well-tended lawns and lives.
So God tells us to improve our lie,
but not to leverage adversity unfairly.
When I ponder the game of golf I'm impressed
by the wonder of God's grace.

God knows we're all duffers,
and grants leeway to adjust to circumstance
without compromising basic principles
or surrendering accountability.

#6 The Short Game

A golfing adage says, "Drive for show, putt for dough."
Sports fans know that many professionals can drive
a golf ball a long distance, often 300 yards or more.
But unless they make accurate short shots
they don't win tournaments.
Short shots are ones that put the ball
onto the green for easy putts.
Duffers take ironic satisfaction watching pros pitch
past the green into a sand trap. Pros, too, are fallible.
They can freeze up when much depends on little.
Missing a putt an inch may cost a hundred thousand bucks.
In life, too, little flubs can be costly. We know this.
In crucial times of life, pressure mounts at closure.
Stress ties our muscles into knots
and short-circuits our brains.
Oh no! We must not blow it! So we pray.
And the Spirit whispers this assurance:
"In quietness and confidence shall be your strength."
Trust in God fixes the eye, steadies the hand,
clears the mind, and purifies the heart,
so that actions, to the best of our abilities,
rightly follow good intention.

#7 Beating Par

In God's kingdom all of us are amateurs,
playing the game of life for the joy of it.
We are Jesus' friends, not his servants,
We won't be dropped from God's tournament.
God isn't a sponsor who makes us wear his cap
and cuts our contract if someone outplays us.
Playing at or below par is a goal, not a mandate.

One sunny August day I scored one under par.
Wow! Next time tho', I went eight over. Typical.
But you know, the playing was fun both times.
The sky was equally beautiful, the rhythm
of walking and swinging just as enjoyable.
And when my wife chipped in a shot
from off the green for a birdie
we both jumped for joy!

God judges by intentions of the heart.
This makes the game of life enjoyable.
This is no license to sin but rather the "good news"
that holiness of heart and life is measured by God's grace—
the earnestness of our faith, not by par performances.
Even end-of-the-day duffers can make it to glory!

#8 Hazards

You should know that golf course designers
don't make things easy, especially for duffers.
Next to a putting green or in the middle of a fairway
they'll scoop out good soil and fill the space with sand.
Or they'll wind a creek through the course and put
a pond right where a golfer's ball might land.
Or they'll take level ground and contour it
in weird ways to make putting harder.
Sand traps and ponds are deliberate efforts
and make par difficult. Aren't trees enough?
Oh, well. I guess art does imitate life,
even in artistic design of golf courses.
Could hazards at play help us cope better
with those real ones we face in daily life?
Actually, hazards to the spirit are far worse
than weedy creeks, ponds, sand traps,
and strangely sloping putting greens.
Coping with hazards to body, mind,
and the spirit is especially difficult
in a world united through technology
but fractured by sin. Maybe overcoming
hazards on the golf course will strengthen us
to use body, mind, and spirit effectively to
cope with real evils. "In the world," said Jesus,
"you will have trouble. But take heart!
I have overcome the world." These words
strengthen me and give me hope!

#9 Good Strokes

Each golf round offers many small satisfactions.
Did you muff a shot or drive the ball into the pond?
Shake it off! Shake if off! Focus on the next stroke.
The total score isn't the only measure of achievement.
Yes, competition sharpens skill. For us duffers, though,
each play has meaning. We don't perform, we play;
and a few good shots can make our day.
When I try too hard, my wife looks at me
and says, "Relax, honey, it's just a game."
So, after praying "thanks, Lord," I feast my eyes
on the scenery, inhale clean air, and resume my play.
Shrugging off worry gives space for something good—
even serendipitous—to occur. Like having a solid approach
shot plunk onto the green and roll into the cup for an eagle!
Or scoring a few par holes and an occasional birdie.

I advocate swinging a golf club with holy joy!
If one is anxious, muscles complain at neurons nagging
them all along the arc of the swing. Just let mind and spirit
trust the body and swing the club with ecstatic abandon!
Golf, like life, is full of ordinary activity and small successes.
Good living is a triumph of spirit, not a scorecard of achievement.
If the eye is fixed wholly on God, our Day on the Course of Life
will be exciting and full of joy. Oh, sure, life isn't a game,
but playfulness can be a virtue for overburdened people.
Joyous trust, not anxiety, is what Jesus teaches.

Tributes to Life in Particular

A Poem

A poem should not be
so mellifluously fat
that the meaning
of the word
is obscured

nor so lean
only skeleton
is seen.

Uncertain Times

"In a jiffy"
is rather iffy;
does it mean soon,
or about noon?

"Wait a sec!"
one may expect,
realistically,
to be hyperbole.

Euphemisms

Euphemisms are great, I feel,
for talking nice instead of naughty;
but take care, they can conceal
the truth, and make us haughty.

Adult Language

"Could you show me?" "Sure, glad to help!" "Thanks!"
"Sorry, my mistake!" "That's okay, we all goof."
"Forgive me, Lord, for I have sinned."
"Is this arrangement fair to everyone?"
"You may be right but this is how I see it."
"The plan is unethical; I'll have no part in it!"
"Until death do us part."
"I love you, sweetheart!"
"Yes, it hurts, but I forgive you."
"We'll work it out together, okay?"
"No thanks, I don't indulge."
"Let's ask God to show us the way."

Adult Entertainment

Loving one's spouse.
Picnicking with the kids.
Tennis, softball, golf, Scrabble.
Travel to interesting places.
Reading books, enjoying music and drama.
Making lap robes for care homes.
Building Habitat for Humanity houses.
Making toys for (someone's) grandchildren.
Walking the beach with Charlie dog.
Enjoying God's glorious sunsets.

A Bit of Fun

There is this historian named Larry,
whose notions are sometimes scary.
Friends, don't be uptight,
he follows Christ the Light—
but must Larry be so contrary?

Staph

There once was a Yachatsian named John,
Whose innards felt quartered and drawn.
Doctors diagnosed it as staph
About which you don't laugh,
Welcome home, John, when it's gone!

Tough Turf Talk

For ignoring, demeaning,
ridiculing, circumventing,
obfuscating and otherwise
rejecting my considered views,
you ignorant clod,
I choose the longest word
in the English language
to label your insouciance:

floccinaucinihilipilification.

The longest word in the English language,
floccinaucinihilipilification *means "to esteem as valueless"*

Homophonic Fun

Aye, aye, I turn my eye to you,
too, my pretty, pretty ewe
grazing beside a stately yew.
Once before there were two,
then four of you, as I recall,
For though one sails the seven seas,
one sees what memory can seize
from visions at first flawed—holey—
then wholly, and finally, holy.
So it's right to write about this rite,
aye, I turn my eye to you,
ewe beside the yew tree!

Mutterings about "Eco-zealotry"

Air head, arrogant babble, balderdash, bilge and
blather, bunkum, claptrap, double-talk drivel,
egocentric eyewash and finessed gabble,
holy hogwash, insensitivity and jabber,
jargon, knavery, little-minded nullity,
obsequious omniscient pap, piffle,
poppycock, prattle and pompous
questing, riposting rigmarole,
silly stuff-and-nonsense,
sycophantic slavering,
tomfoolery, twaddle,
usurious unction,
vacuous villainy,
wacky, x-ed out,
yucky and
zilch.
Zero?
Yes, but
X-rayed by
virtue, vexed
until very tired,
thankful for small
satisfactions, reaching
for rescue, quiescent and
praying, overborne by onerous
ostentation, napalmed by naughty
meddling—matched meekly—lofting
latitude to live kindly, if not kingly, with
justice and joy instead of insults, hoping
to honor God's generous gifts, finding folks
faithful everywhere, earnest, doing their duty
conscientious, caring, believing, affirming their
allegiance to the One above, all the way—Z to A!

Memories

Memories surge from out the past
like a long wake that trails
a ship slowing toward
the Port.

Innocency at Lunch

Skinny, fuzzy, brown legs dangle
from the stool where she sits (sort of)
eating a MacDonald's hamburger.
An in-fashion strand of hair
curls down over her T-shirt.
The cuisine isn't spectacular,
but, framed in human perspective,
the picture certainly is.

Five Quick Queries

Have you smelled sagebrush in the morning after rain?
How long ago did you drink water from a spring?
Your hands, what gratifying memories do they hold?
Your ears, what satisfying words have they been told?
Did you ever see an eagle on the wing?

1993

Blue Jeans

I speak in praise of blue jeans:
honest apparel, congenial
to all sorts of human activity;
forthrightly conformable
to male and female anatomy;
inexpensive and appealing.

I give tribute to blue jeans:
comfortable and universal;
democracy's defense against tyranny,
neatly nonconscriptable;
flags to a global destiny
the people are unfurling.

The Soil Gives Birth

Why does the sunlight seem to tarry?
Why does a lingering blanket of cold
tenaciously hug the restless earth?
Here's why—and it's a tale oft told—
the earth is pregnant, about to birth.
(With a precious burden, one is wary!)

We name this waiting, February.

Don't be impatient, don't be weary,
the earth is strong and very bold,
delivery comes. Surely the worth
of waiting outweighs pure gold.
At full term the soil gives birth
to flowers and fruit, root and berry.

Oh, what joy hope can carry!

The Blahs

Fear the February blahs,
pedagogical blahs!
What monotony their melancholy tells!
How they rumble, rumble, rumble
in the foggy air of night!
While the clouds that over stumble
the semester, seem to tumble
with a blasé, malaiséd blight
our academic time, time, time,
into a numbly static clime,
a discombobulation that so miserably gnaws
at us within the blahs, blahs, blahs,
blahs, blahs, blahs—
within the plodding and the nodding of the blahs.

with acknowledgments to Edgar Allen Poe

Fickle February

All lovers of earth, be wary;
nothing's as fickle as February.

One day a sharp voice may regale
beach houses with a sudden freeze
or, laughing in raucous gale,
shatter the joy of budding trees,
filling their outstretched arms,
not with warmth, but ice.
This embrace signals alarms;
it's naughty, and not nice.

Don't phone the constabulary,
other moods has February.

Lovers often are blessed twice,
for fickleness also charms:
A soft, warm rain will suffice
to quicken growth on all the farms,
and sunshine offers to the bees
(and to us) hopes that do entail
sweet promises, to tease
the heart. Such love will not fail.

Green Hopes

The days drizzle minutes
with dull, grey disdain
for my restless spirit.
Miserly February!

I want a generous sun
to lavish my hours
and days with wonder
at what light brings.

I even welcome those
interludes of rain
that burnish golden
the tips of things,

things that burst silent
through warmed soil,
making my hopes
green, inflationary.

1991

Apocalypse or Peace?

Winter storms are quite contrary,
northern gales bring drifting snow
and east winds strike a chilling blow.
Seasonal winds certainly vary,
whenever the date says February.
Weather quickly can change its show,
for west winds can be arbitrary
and southern gusts can make things grow.

This year storms swirl desert sand
from west to east, from south to north,
lashing every loved homeland.
Apocalypse or peace, which course
will the nations' weather take?
What changes will the Spirit make?

At the Hint of Gold

What is as sure as death and taxes?
What as certain as ebbing tides?
Predictable as the common cold?
This: a dull grey gloom that slides
like sluggish slime into the soul
and dutifully attacks us.

We name this monster, February.

What is as sure as birth and taxes?
As determined as the flooding tides?
Predictable as a tale retold?
It is that the foggy phantom glides
away at earth's first hint of gold—
How quickly its grip relaxes,

Oh, divine apothecary!

Prayer at Neptune's Rounding

Lord God, a dozen years ago
we strapped bands of logic
around refashioned stuff,
tapped into your power line, and
launched our creation into space.
With playful electronic fingers
we have traced its trajectories
past Jupiter, Saturn, Uranus.
We delighted in exotic vistas
found along expanding horizons.
Voyager 2 has quickened our hopes
without quite defining them.

Soon Voyager will round Neptune
and snap its tether to humanity.
Will these hopes for a bright future
be dashed by closer vistas of violence,
hunger, pollution, and exploitation?
We don't need another expensive
monument to human failure.
Lord, we have launched a seed of hope
into the womb of time. Nurture it!
Guide its deep journey!
Plant the seed firmly in our future,
Prepare us for your cosmic kingdom.
Amen.

Voyager 2 was launched in 1977, rounded Neptune August 24, 1989, then escaped the solar system for a long odyssey through the Milky Way galaxy.

Tributes to God's Grace

Children's Prayers at Dawn

1.

No scary dreams last night, Lord.
Thanks, too, for the morning sun
that wakes me and warms my room,
and for my mama and my papa,
who await me at the kitchen table,
with cornbread and cocoa—and kisses.
I'm not afraid to ride the bus anymore!
Please take good care of Skippy dog;
he gets lonely when I'm at school.
In Jesus' name, amen.

2.

Thank you, God, for helping me
be kind to my sister today
instead of hitting her
when she took my crayons
and scribbled on my book.
Mama says I should be like Jesus.
I want to, but sometimes I forget,
or don't know how.
Help me, Lord. Amen.

3.

Lord, in Sunday School today
we learned about Jesus and
that little big shot Zacchaeus,
who scrambled up a tree—
better to see the Master.
People must have laughed to see
a grown man climb a tree!
I'm glad Jesus didn't laugh at him
but went to his house for dinner.
I like it that pushy old Zacchaeus
promised to quit cheating folks,
and to pay them back! Amen

Your Hand Leading Me

Lord, it's hard to distinguish
what I want from what I need.
At the mall luxuries look like necessities;
back home I know my needs are deeper.
Clothes and fancy gadgets aren't enough.
Help me see things through your eyes, Jesus.
Cruciform love puts things in perspective.
What I really hope for is unfailing love,
satisfying tasks, friendships, health, peace,
reassurance of your gracious promises—
forgiveness, holiness, joy—
and your hand leading me
into life eternal. Amen.

Guilt

Lord, I cope with it during the day,
looking people straight in the eye,
talking confidently, doing my work well.
I cleverly board all flights of thought
that rationalize my actions.

I am good at covering up.
But when I'm alone guilt swarms
around me like flies at a picnic.
Surely others can spot that guilt
in my eyes and in my face.

Do they notice the tremor
of conscience in my hands
and in my speech? At night
truth penetrates the facade.
Your arrows pierce my armor.

I give up, Lord. I plead guilty.
Be merciful to me, a sinner.

In Jesus' name, amen.

Confession

Lord, I understand confession
is good for the soul. So here it is.
For one thing, I talk too much:
adroitly shoving others aside
to gain center of attention.
I say and do dumb things;
I clown around and poke fun
at other folks—a boorish critic.
Actually, I'm the one laughed at,
the wacky, bumbling one.

I'm disappointed in myself.
I'm concerned about my reputation,
so I scrounge for public approval
instead of seeking truth about myself.

Deliver me from stupidity, Lord,
so I won't feel ashamed anymore.
Forgive me. Heal me. Love me.
Help me converse graciously
with neighbors and friends,
to love others, and myself,
with integrity.

Amen.

Deliver Me

Lord, I was tempted today and almost succumbed.
Even though in principle the action is wrong,
in this particular case it seemed right.
The tempter came as an angel of light.
He beguiled me—subtle con artist!
I wanted both to yield and to resist.
A pleasant image of the temptation
lingers at the doorway of my mind.
Fortunately your Spirit checked me.
Speak up, Lord. I can barely hear
your voice over the static in my soul!
In your wisdom, reveal more clearly
the ugly underside of this sin
that so tempted me.
Deliver me from the evil one!

Amen.

I'm Lonely

Lord, I am lonely.
Oh, I know what *should* be done.
I should seek out a neighbor
for friendly conversation,
or write a letter, or telephone
a dear neglected loved one.
But I let the thought die.

I am afraid I'll be rebuffed,
gently. People are busy.
I'm butting into their lives.
Their smiles indulge me.
They're just being polite.
I feel superfluous. At least
that's what I tell myself.

I want others to find me!
And so my thoughts idle.
I surf a few TV programs,
start and quit a mystery novel.
I'm lonely, Lord. Hold me close.
Whisper words of comfort
Assure me of your love.

Amen.

Nudged into Shadows

Lilies flourish and grass grows lush.
But a cold wind shrivels new sprouts;
busy birds break tender buds
and careless feet trample
and scuff the tender grass.

I feel that way sometimes, Lord,
shriveled, broken, trampled upon.
Faith's glow fades as I seek the sun,
only to be nudged into shadows
by ones stronger than I.

Lord, my roots are well watered,
but I need light, I need warmth,
protection. Lord, hear my cry.
Strengthen me. Empower me.

Amen.

Dreams

I had disturbing dreams
last night and woke up tired.
In my dream I couldn't get home:
At every turn obstacles rose up
and trapped me in a maze.
Vicious dogs charged at me,
and in terror I kicked out at
these nighttime beasts.

Sometimes I enjoy good dreams—
leaping effortlessly over mountains.
I wish these came more often.
Do these dreams mean anything, Lord,
or are their strange scenarios
just patterns of an idling brain,
keeping up my pulse rate?
Speak to my confusion.

Reveal your presence now
and in my troubled nights. Lord,
enter my darkness, my dreams.
Where there is sin, reveal it.
Where there is hurt, heal it.
Where there is doubt, give faith.
I will be guided by your Spirit.
Thank you, Lord.

Amen.

In the Soil of Grace

It has not been a good day, Lord.
I had expected commendation
but got criticized instead.
I'm disappointed in friends,
in my country, in the church,
kinfolk, and (it's hard to admit)
I'm disappointed in myself.

Expectations outstrip performance.
A chasm separates the ideal
from the real world. Tell me
again about unconditional love,
about how your Spirit works
in the world. Restore my vision
of the kingdom present now.

Bridge my expectation gap.
Help me be more loving
and less censorious.
Keep me from sulking
and from waxing cynical.
Plant my hopes once more
in the soil of your grace.

Amen.

Heavenly Fire

Lord, candles on young pines trees
have reached seasonal growth.
With warming days, green needles
throw off drab winter wraps
to bask joyously in the sun.

Oh, Lord, that's how I feel.
Verdant beneath your love,
oozing juices of the Holy Spirit,
reaching open-armed to the sky.
I sing glory, glory, glory!

But springtime ecstasy
makes me vulnerable
to chilling nighttime winds
and seductive predators.
I can be hurt and damaged.

And so I stretch myself
toward you, oh, my Lord.
Your heavenly fire warms me.
Your truth strengthens me.
Your love nurtures me.

I sing glory, glory, glory!

Amen.

Thank You, Lord

Thank you for good food
and a comfortable house.
Thank you for family and friends,
for satisfying tasks, and good health.
Thank you for the beauty of your creation
and for the world of ideas and things
which people—made in your image—
have created. Help me enjoy what I possess
without coveting things I do not own.
Teach me to enjoy what belongs
to everyone: sunsets, ocean beaches,
forests, storms, sunshine.
And, everywhere, children at play.
Thank you, Lord!

Amen.

Teach Us, Lord

Teach us, Lord, your ways of peace.
Within the home direct our hands,
our words, O Christ of Galilee.
Let our home heed your command
to love—a kingdom province be.
Teach us not to build on sand
but to build on rock faithfully.
From all fears give full release;
in your truth, by grace, we stand.
Teach us, Lord, your ways of peace.

Teach us, Lord, your ways of peace.
At work and in the marketplace
where money is exchanged, and speech,
and goods, let us see your face.
May we be fair, Lord, each to each.
Let love leave everywhere a trace
of Golgotha. May justice reach
to everyone so wars may cease
and we are one, by your grace.
Teach us, Lord, your ways of peace.

Teach us, Lord, your ways of peace,
within the structures of the state
in which we share a common life.

From lies and prejudice and hate,
from tyrannies of left and right
deliver us. Teach us to await
love's sure victory over strife,
to labor so that wars may cease.
Your kingdom in our midst create.
Teach us, Lord, your ways of peace.

Teach us, Lord, your ways of peace
within the church: For this we pray.
Together we will truly bring
our lives to you. Lord, lead the way.
O Christ, be prophet, priest, and king,
so once again the world may say,
"They really love each other." Sing,
yes, sing with us of love's increase,
the end of war, of your new day.
Teach us, Lord, your ways of peace.

Timely Words from Jesus

Verse One:

Christians, are you listening?
Are you hearing what I say?
Hasn't God forgiven you—
who are you to cast a stone?
Is God's grace for you alone?
Earth is but a common land,
and I have other sheep, you know,
who are not within your fold.

Verse Two:

Christians, are you listening?
Are you hearing what I say?
Give to those who ask in need,
and, lending, do not yield to greed.
Are your enemies impoverished?
Feed them, go the second mile—
good for evil—do not kill,
or even hate, but love them.

Verse Three:

Christians, are you listening?
Are you hearing what I say?
Feed the hungry in my name,
clothe the naked, heal the lame;
take the homeless stranger in,
and visit the imprisoned ones.
When you show such love to others,
you show your love to me.

Chorus:

Why do you call me, Lord,
and not do what I say?
Christians of the world,
are you building on the sand,
or building on the Rock?

Christ in Christmas

"Seasons greetings!" cheerfully affirms
friends and family in wintertime.
It serves equally well
in summer or in spring,
or even in the fall.
One size fits all.

"Merry Christmas!"
is more time specific;
it's rightly honorific,
synchronous with bells rung,
manger scenes, and carols sung,
celebrating God's great gift—Jesus.

"Merry Christmas!"

To Join the Great Throng

(to be sung to the Welsh melody "St. Denio")

Verse One:

Lord Jesus, your promise of eternal life
relieves us of fear in this time of great strife.
Sustain us and keep us from falling in sin
and guide us each day by your Spirit within.

Verse Two:

Though tempted and tested we will not despair,
we know you are with us; we know that you care.
We'll witness the gospel at home and abroad,
in word and in deed so that all may know God.

Verse Three:

O Jesus, we ask you to shield us from pride
in things we accomplish—or devils defied.
May love be our aim in whatever we do,
Your kingdom the standard to which we are true.

Verse Four:

Lord Jesus, when death comes to knock at the door
receive us in heaven for life evermore.
O glory, O glory, to join that great throng
in praise to our God with a jubilant song!

2002

Let There Be Light!

God said, "Let there be Light!"
and from this space/time word,
in a billion billionth of a second,
the cosmos burst forth and packed
dark nothingness with bright energy
configured into star-filled galaxies,
in one of which (at least) a small planet
swarmed with living creatures, including
humanity stamped with divine likeness,
intelligent, purposeful, testing the boundaries
of freedom to be co-creators with God.
The recorded struggle reveals a mixture
of good and evil, the joyous and the tragic.

Again God said, "Let there be Light!"
and through the womb of a woman
in an obscure Mediterranean village,
a Child burst into our space/time world.
God's word made flesh dwelt among us.
We name this word Jesus, whose brightness
dispels the darkness of human sin
and portends a cosmos resplendent
with unimaginable glory as we creatures,
crafted in the divine image, choose
to build by the Creator's blueprint.
Does this Word, this Light, still shine?
Sure it does! Oh yes! Yes! Yes!

Wrapped in Cloth

Wrapping a gift in paper
demonstrates our intent
to magnify an act of love,
beautifully and suitably,
to keep eyes from spoiling
the glory of a moment
when unwrapping the gift
unites giver and recipient
in a covenant of peace.

God wrapped his gift in cloth—
beautifully simple, suitably
disguised from Herod's eyes.
Joyfully we join shepherds,
angels, magi, and the stars
to treasure, to savor the time
in history and in the heart
when unwrapping this gift
united us with the Giver
in a covenant of peace.

Epilogue

The Good, the True, and the Beautiful

A path winds through a forest not far from here,
so well-traveled it is that dirt in places
has been polished to high gloss, like a pew
that has known decades of caressing hands.

On either side ancient trees rise to meet sunlight.
Some were planted there with hope and purpose,
others have sprung up wild with hope and passion.

Though cast in shadows here and there, the path is suffused
with permanence and wisdom: a place that encourages
barks of laughter and celebration, tempered with
that solemn respect one feels in any place of worship.

The path is long with inclines and descents, and places
that fold back upon each other so that one can never see
far into the distance. Yet the path goes on, through terrain
that only as yet can be imagined, anticipation building.

Generations will walk this path, the older ones seeking solace
and answers for their own confusions and disappointments,
some merely looking for fresh air and God's grace.

Youngsters will just run and play, captivated here and there
by a pretty flower or a strange bug, not yet stopping to question
why this place feels so right and true, not yet understanding
the precious gift, a legacy bestowed.

This path, tended with love, has been worn smooth
through the experiences of two lives intertwined,
searching out the good, the true, and the beautiful
in this earthly place.

by our granddaughter Robin Shepard
2007

www.ingramcontent.com/pod-product-compliance
Lightning Source LLC
La Vergne TN
LVHW050646100826
845148LV00011B/2000

* 9 7 8 1 5 9 4 9 8 0 1 1 4 *